This item was donated to
**Spalding University
Book Review Center**
through the generosity of

Oxford University
Press

SPALDING UNIVERSITY
LIBRARY

SIGNS OF THE TIMES

THE STORY OF COMMUNICATONS

by Anita Ganeri

Oxford University Press

Published in the United States by
Oxford University Press
198 Madison Avenue
New York, NY 10016

Oxford is a registered trademark of Oxford University Press, Inc.

Published in the United Kingdom by
Evans Brothers Limited
2A Portman Mansions
Chiltern Street
London W1M 1LE

© copyright Evans Brothers Limited 1997

All Rights Reserved. No part of this publication may be reproduced, stored in a retrieval system or transmitted in any form, or by any means, electronic, mechanical, photocopying, recording or otherwise, without prior permission of Evans Brothers Limited.

First published 1997

Printed in Hong Kong by Wing King Tong Co. Ltd

Acknowledgments
Editor: Nicola Barber
Design: Neil Sayer
Production: Jenny Mulvanny
With thanks to Ian Graham, who acted as consultant on this title, and to Malcolm Jones of the Esperanto-Asocio de Britio, who provided the translation on page 11.

Library of Congress Cataloging-in-Publication Data
Ganeri, Anita, 1961-
  The story of communications / Anita Ganeri
    p. cm.—(Signs of the times)
  Includes index.
  1. Communication and traffic—History—Juvenile literature. [1. Communication—History.] I. Title. II. Series: Ganeri, Anita, 1961- Signs of the times.
HE152.G26 1997
384—dc21   97-30691
                                                    CIP
                                                    AC

ISBN 0-19-521411-0

Acknowledgments
Cover (top left) Science Museum/Science and Society Picture Library (top right) e.t archive (bottom left) Last Resort Picture Library (bottom right) Science Museum/Science and Society Picture Library (main image) Robert Harding Picture Library Back cover Trip/H Rogers
Title page J-L Charmet/Science Photo Library page 6 (top) Marc Grimberg/Image Bank (bottom) NMPFT/Science and Society Picture Library page 7 (top) Bruce Forster/Tony Stone (bottom) Robert Harding Picture Library page 8 (top) National Maritime Museum, London (bottom) Mark Green/Getty Images page 9 (top) Blair Seitz/Science Photo Library (bottom) Mark Pidgeon/Oxford Scientific Films page 10 (top) Renee Lynn/Getty Images (bottom) Robert Harding Picture Library page 11 (left) Corbis-Bettmann (right) Val Corbett/Getty Images page 12 British Museum/Bridgeman Art Library page 13 (top left) South American Pictures (bottom left) Tony Morrison/South American Pictures (bottom right) Getty Images page 14 (top) Mercury Archives/Image Bank (bottom) Peter Newark's Western Americana page 15 (top) Robert Harding Picture Library (bottom left) U.S Postal Service (bottom right) Getty Images page 16 (top) Leonard de Selva/Corbis (bottom) Science Museum/Science and Society Picture Library page 17 (top and bottom) Science Museum/Science and Society Picture Library page 18 (left) Getty Images (right) Corbis-Bettmann/UPI page 19 (top) J-L Charmet/Science Photo Library (bottom left) Trip/Viesti (bottom right) Science Museum/Science and Society Picture Library page 20 BBC Photograph Library (bottom) Francoise Sauze/Science Photo Library page 21 (top) Rex Features (middle) Orde Eliason/Link (bottom) Trip/H Rogers page 22 (top) Image Bank (bottom) NMPFT/Science and Society Picture Library page 23 (top) Getty Images (bottom) Orde Eliason/Link page 24 (left) Getty Images (right) NASA/Science and Society Picture Library page 25 (top) Tony Buxton/Science Photo Library (bottom) Bob Strong/Rex Features page 26 (top) James King-Holmes/Science Photo Library (bottom) Gaillard, Jerrican/Science Photo Library page 27 (top and bottom) Rex Features page 28 (top) Science Museum/Science and Society Picture Library (bottom) Trip/H Rogers

Contents

KEEPING IN TOUCH

Messages in and out	6
Signals and symbols	8
The spoken word	10

IN THE MAIL

Letter writing	12

TELECOMMUNICATIONS

Talking telegraph	16
Telephone calls	18
On the radio	20
Television takes over	22

MODERN COMMUNICATIONS

Satellites and computers	24
Into the future	26
Timeline	28
Glossary	29
Index	30

KEEPING IN TOUCH

MESSAGES IN AND OUT

Every day, all day, you send and receive messages. There are many ways of doing this. You might use your voice, make a face, or gesture with your hands. You might read a magazine or newspaper, write a letter, watch television, or make a phone call. These are all types of communication – ways of sending and sharing information with other people, whether over short distances, to the other side of the world, or even to outer space.

THE PRINTED WORD

At school and at home, you are surrounded by examples of writing and printing. Books, magazines, newspapers, and advertisements keep you informed and entertained. The printed word is one of the most powerful and widespread forms of communication, able to reach many millions of people every day.

Newspapers are one of the most important forms of communication. Millions of papers are sold every day.

A 1902 Box Brownie camera. Advances in photography have helped to revolutionize communications.

BREAKTHROUGH

Many of the forms of communication in use today would not exist without the amazing advances that have taken place in technology. The invention of writing, printing, and photography, the discovery of electricity, and the incredible steps forward in space technology have made worldwide communications possible.

TELECOMMUNICATIONS

Telecommunications are ways of sending messages using electricity. They include the telegraph, telephone, radio, and television. In the 1990s mobile phones, or cellular phones, have become very popular. A mobile phone is a cross between a walkie-talkie and a telephone. It uses batteries and does not have cords or wires, so it is light and easy to carry around.

REACHING THE WORLD

In the last 30 years satellites and computers have revolutionized communications. You can now communicate with someone on the other side of the world in a matter of seconds. Satellite television (see page 24) began in 1983. On January 28, 1996, a record audience of 138.5 million people watched Super Bowl XXX, which was shown on satellite TV.

A mobile phone is the latest way of keeping in touch while you are on the move. Mobile phones first became available in the 1980s.

A prehistoric horse, painted on a wall in the Lascaux caves in France

IN FACT...

Some of the earliest forms of communication are pictures painted by prehistoric people. The oldest, found in caves in Spain and France, date from more than 20,000 years ago. Most of these pictures show animals such as bison, mammoths, horses, and deer. It is thought they were painted to tell a story, such as that of a good hunting trip, or to bring luck in a hunt.

Signals and Symbols

For thousands of years, people have used signals and symbols to communicate with one another. Signals are particularly useful for sending messages between people who can see each other but who are out of hearing range. Both signals and symbols allow people to communicate even if they do not speak the same language.

The famous flag message sent at the Battle of Trafalgar

BURNING BRIGHT
The ancient Greeks and Romans used burning torches to pass on military messages. They waved, raised, or lowered the torches a set number of times for different letters of the alphabet. The message was passed on, from watchtower to watchtower, by teams of signalers. The Greeks also used mirrors to flash coded messages by reflecting the rays of the sun.

FLYING THE FLAG
Before radio was invented, ships used code flags to communicate at sea. Each flag stood for a letter. One of the most famous flag messages ever sent came from Lord Nelson's ship, HMS *Victory*, at the Battle of Trafalgar in 1805. The flags read "England expects that every man will do his duty."

SPOTTING SYMBOLS
Some symbols are used for identification, such as those on flags, and some to give instructions, such as those on road signs. They provide a great deal of information in a simple, direct way and are easy to recognize. For example, the five interlocking circles on the Olympic flag stand for the five continents of the world, united in sport.

The Olympic flag

CODED MESSAGE

A code is a way of sending a secret message by using signs or symbols, including letters, to stand for letters and words. People have been writing in code for thousands of years. An ancient example from Iraq dates from about 1500 B.C. Read normally, this text is a poem of 27 verses, giving advice on religious matters. But the first letters of each verse contain a coded message – the name of the author and details about his life and background.

BODY LANGUAGE

The way you sit, stand, or use your hands, and the faces that you make can tell other people a great deal about you. Your body language shows if you are feeling happy, sad, nervous, confident … often without your even knowing it! Body language can also help the police tell if suspects are lying or telling the truth.

SIGNPOST

Deaf people use a special language, based on hand and arm movements, and facial expressions. It is called sign language, and it was pioneered by a French priest, Charles de l'Epée, in the 18th century. Different countries have their own sign language, just as they have their own spoken language.

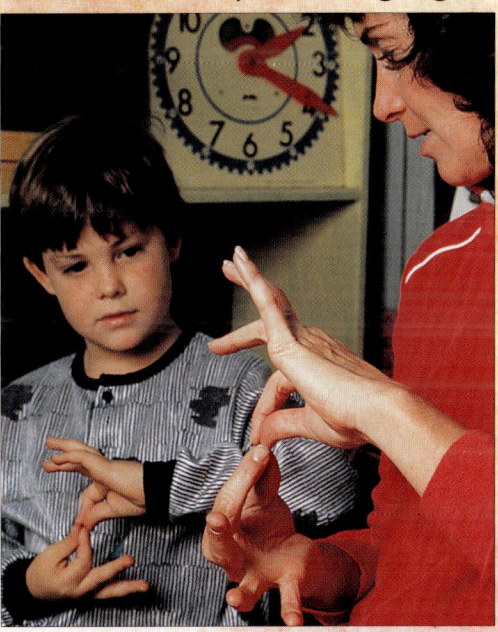

Learning how to use sign language

IN FACT…

Like humans, animals have many ways of communicating with one another. They use songs, sounds, colors, patterns, smells, and movement to keep in touch. Ring-tailed lemurs have long striped tails (left). When a group of lemurs is searching for food on the ground, all the lemurs keep their tails raised high in the air, like flags. This helps to keep the group together.

THE SPOKEN WORD

For centuries, sending messages by word of mouth was the main way of recording and passing on pieces of information. The only problem with this system was that it was not always very reliable. After all, some messengers had much better memories than others! To this day, the spoken word remains our most common form of communication.

FIRST SPEAKERS
Scientists think that until about 40,000 years ago, people's skulls and voice boxes were the wrong shape to make the sounds used today. Instead, people "talked" with grunts and gestures. Language as we know it may have begun with people imitating natural sounds, such as animal noises and the moaning of the wind.

BREAKTHROUGH

Writing was invented about 5,500 years ago, thousands of years after language developed. It provided a more dependable way of sending messages. People could keep accurate records, accounts, and histories and pass on news and ideas more reliably. Some of the earliest examples of writing come from Sumeria (Iraq). Carved on clay tablets, small picture symbols were used to represent words.

HOW MANY LANGUAGES?
About 3,950 languages and dialects are spoken in the world today, some 845 of these in India. The most common language is Chinese, spoken by more than 1 billion people. Next comes English, with about 800 million speakers.

Early people may have imitated natural sounds, such as the howl of a wolf.

Building the Tower of Babel. According to the Bible, this was the beginning of the world's great variety of languages.

WHISTLES AND CLICKS

The people of La Gomera, one of the Canary Islands, use Spanish and a whistled language, called *silbo*, to talk to one another. The island is very hilly, so it is easier to whistle a message to people living in the next valley than to walk for several hours to speak to them. The sounds carry so well that they can be heard up to 5 miles (8 kilometers) away. Several African languages use clicking sounds for some consonants. The clicks are made with the tongue, lips, and cheeks.

BOOKS OF WORDS

One of the earliest dictionaries with the words arranged in alphabetical order was put together by a Roman writer, Verrius Flaccus, in the 1st century A.D. It was called *De Verborum Significatu* (The Meaning of Words). The largest English-language dictionary is the 20-volume *Oxford English Dictionary*. It has 21,700 pages and contains about 231,000 main-word entries.

The hilly landscape of La Gomera in the Canary Islands. The people of La Gomera use a whistled language to communicate from one valley to the next.

The English writer Dr. Samuel Johnson (1709-84) produced the first comprehensive dictionary of the English language in 1755.

SIGNPOST

For centuries, people have tried to invent a world language that everyone on Earth could speak and understand. At least 600 "universal" languages have been suggested. In 1887, a Polish eye specialist named Dr. Ludwig Zamenhof invented Esperanto. Esperanto means "hopeful" and it is based largely on Latin, Greek, German, and Italian. Although a million textbooks have been sold and about 10 million people have learned to speak Esperanto, it has never really caught on.

ESPERANTO TEASER

Can you figure out which well-known nursery rhyme this is?

Brilu, brilu, eta stel',
Vi mirigas sur ĉiel'.
Alte super mond', kaj for –
Kiel diamant' aŭ or'.

Answer: *Twinkle, twinkle little star*

IN THE MAIL

LETTER WRITING

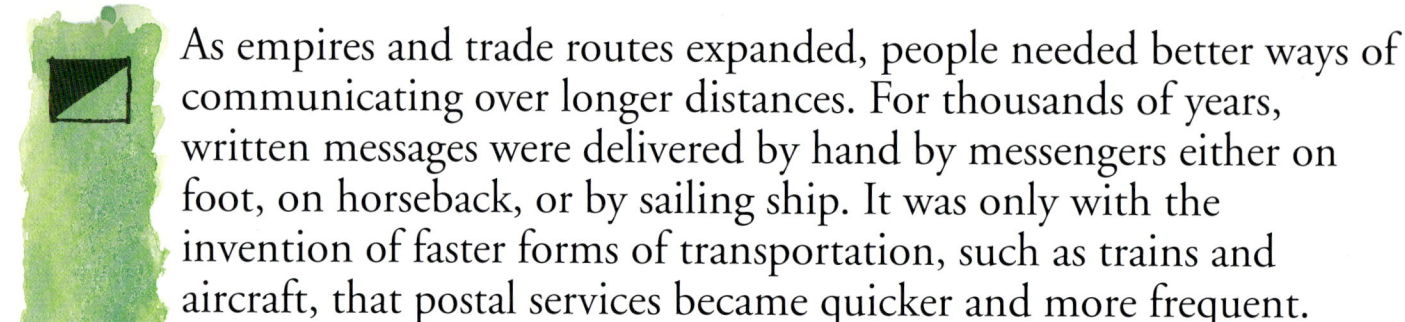

As empires and trade routes expanded, people needed better ways of communicating over longer distances. For thousands of years, written messages were delivered by hand by messengers either on foot, on horseback, or by sailing ship. It was only with the invention of faster forms of transportation, such as trains and aircraft, that postal services became quicker and more frequent.

FIRST POSTAL SERVICE

The Assyrians of ancient Iraq had a very efficient postal service almost 4,000 years ago. Letters were written on small clay tablets and placed inside clay envelopes.

ROMAN MAIL

The Roman postal services, the *cursus publicus*, was set up by Emperor Augustus in the 1st century B.C. It was for official use only. Through a vast network of messengers, post offices, and ships, the emperor kept in touch with the farthest parts of the Roman Empire.

PIGEON MAIL

Both the ancient Greeks and Romans used birds to carry messages. The Greeks used pigeons to send everything from love letters to lists of results from the Olympic Games. Wealthy Romans sent the chariot-racing results from Rome to their country estates by swallow! Well-trained birds were worth a fortune. The first people to use pigeons may have been the Egyptians in the 12th century B.C., to carry military instructions.

Hunting birds, a scene from an ancient Egyptian wall painting. The ancient Egyptians also used birds to carry messages.

IN FACT...

A royal postal service was first established in China in about 1000 B.C. Messengers rode on horseback and were famous for their speed. Feathers were attached to important letters to mark them as urgent!

INCA RELAYS

The Incas of South America built a great network of roads to link their vast empire. The two main roads were a coast road, 250 miles (400 kilometers) long, and the royal road, which ran for 3,225 miles (5,200 kilometers) through the rugged Andes Mountains. Government runners, called *chasquis*, were stationed at 2-mile (3-kilometer) intervals along the roads. They carried messages or packages in relays, to and from the royal court. A team of runners could cover 200 miles (320 kilometers) a day. Each runner carried a conch shell trumpet, which he blew to warn the next man that he was coming. The runners waited in small shelters built by the side of the road.

An Inca chasquis, *or relay runner, blows his conch shell trumpet to alert the next runner.*

Cuzco lies high in the Andes Mountains of Peru. It was the Inca's capital city and lay at the center of their vast empire. Teams of runners carried messages from the royal court in Cuzco to all parts of the empire.

BREAKTHROUGH

One of the greatest breakthroughs in the history of communications happened in Europe in the 15th century. This was the invention of printing. Printing was actually first used in China many centuries before, but the technology did not reach the West. Before the 15th century, every letter and book produced in Europe had to be written out by hand. With the invention of printing, however, books and newsletters could be produced more cheaply and in greater numbers, reaching more people than they ever could before.

An early printing press

13

PUBLIC SERVICE

The first postal services were established to help rulers govern their empires and kingdoms. Only government officials were allowed to use them. There was little demand for postal services for the public because few people could read or write. Then, in the 1300s, merchants in Europe set up their own courier services. In 1627, the French government opened public post offices in many major cities and fixed the postal rates.

The "ladies window" at an early post office

PONY EXPRESS

In the 18th and 19th centuries, most letters were carried on horseback or in horse-drawn coaches. In 1860, a fast and efficient postal service began in the United States. It was known as the Pony Express. Teams of riders galloped in relays across the countryside. It took 240 hours to carry mail 1,960 miles (3,165 kilometers). Riders rode for 100 miles (160 kilometers) at a stretch, stopping every 15 miles (25 kilometers) to change horses. Only one bag of mail was ever lost!

STEAMING AHEAD

The development in the mid-19th century of more modern means of transportation, such as steam trains and steamships, made transporting mail quicker and more reliable. Letters were first carried by train in 1830, between Liverpool and Manchester in England. Postal clerks sorted the mail while the trains chugged across the countryside. When passing through a station, the clerks tossed sacks of sorted mail from the moving train on to the railway platform.

MOST MAIL

The country that handles the most mail is the United States. Over 170 billion letters and packages are mailed each year and the U.S. Postal Service employs some 700,000 people. India is the country with the most post offices – about 150,000.

The first Pony Express rider leaves St. Joseph, Missouri, on April 3, 1860

SIGNPOST

The world's first pre-paid, stick-on postage stamps were issued in Britain in 1840. Only two types were made: the penny black and the two-penny blue. For a penny, a half-ounce (14-gram) letter could be delivered anywhere in the country. Before this, the amount paid to mail a letter was based on the distance it had to travel and the number of pages it contained. Postage was paid by the person receiving the letter, not by the sender.

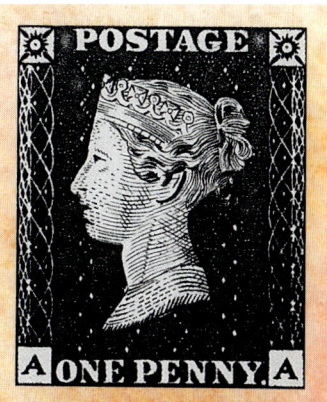

A penny black stamp

LOST IN THE MAIL

A letter delivered to a woman in Switzerland in 1978 was more than 27 years late! It was one of 60 found in a mailbag 3,840 feet (1,200 meters) up on the slopes of Mont Blanc in France. The plane carrying the mail had crashed in the mountains in 1950.

In a modern sorting office, computers are used to sort letters into districts for delivery.

BREAKTHROUGH

The invention of powered flight in 1903 meant that letters could be sent by air for the first time. The first regular airmail service began in 1919, flying letters between England and France. Today, airmail letters usually take only a few days to reach the other side of the world.

Unloading mail from the first airmail flight from Australia to England in 1931

TELECOMMUNICATIONS
TALKING TELEGRAPH

Telecommunications – the telegraph, telephone, radio, and television – all use electricity to work. They change information into signals that can be sent over long distances, through wires, by radio waves, or through optical fibers (see page 19). The first type of electric communication was the telegraph, which was invented in the early 19th century.

Chappe's mechanical telegraph

MOVING ARMS
In the 1790s, a French priest and engineer named Claude Chappe invented a mechanical telegraph. It used a network of hilltop towers, placed 3 to 6 miles (5 to 10 kilometers) apart, between Paris and other French cities. Each tower had arms that could be moved into different positions to spell out different letters. The operator in the next tower copied the message and passed it on.

BREAKTHROUGH

In an electric telegraph, letters are translated into code. The code is sent as bursts of electricity along wires. This type of communication was only made possible in the 18th century when scientists discovered how to make electricity flow along wires. This is called current electricity.

MORSE CODE
The main drawback with early electric telegraphs was that each letter of the alphabet used a separate wire. In 1844, an American named Samuel Morse invented a simple, single-wire telegraph. Each letter was represented by a series of dots and dashes, known as Morse code. For example, • - is *a*, - ••• is *b*, and - • - • is *c*. The operator tapped out the message in dots and dashes by pressing a switch. At the receiver's end, the pattern of dots and dashes was traced on to a paper tape, ready to be decoded.

A Morse tapper

16

RAILWAY SIGNALS

By the 1860s, the telegraph had become the main means of long-distance communication. Telegraph lines linked most big cities. At telegraph offices, people paid to send telegrams. A telegram was transmitted to another office, then delivered by hand. The railways were quick to take up the telegraph, to keep track of trains. Before this, stations had little idea where trains were at any given time.

GOING UNDERWATER

Telegraphs needed wires or cables to send messages. For telegrams to be sent abroad, cables had to be laid under the sea. The first successful transatlantic (across the Atlantic) telegraph cable was laid, by the *Great Eastern* steamship, in 1866. For the first time, telegrams could be sent between Europe and the United States.

IN FACT...

The world's first public telegraph service was installed in England in 1843. Two years later, it was used to catch a murderer! A man killed a woman in Slough, then boarded a train for London. The Slough police promptly sent a telegram to their London colleagues, who arrested the man when he stepped off the train at the other end.

The early telegraph used to catch the Slough murderer

The Great Eastern *on its way to lay the Atlantic telegraph cable*

TELEPHONE CALLS

In the early 1900s, the telephone took over from the telegraph as the most important way of keeping in touch. Today, it is hard to imagine life without it! Like the telegraph, a telephone uses electricity flowing along wires, but it sends actual sounds instead of codes. When you speak into the phone, the receiver turns your voice into an electric current. At the other end, the current is changed back into sound.

SIGNPOST

The first words spoken by telephone were "Mr. Watson, come here, I want you!" on March 10, 1876. A Scottish doctor, Alexander Graham Bell (below), was working on a new type of telegraph. He had spilled some acid on his clothes and was calling for his assistant. This proved, for the first time, that sound could be sent along wires.

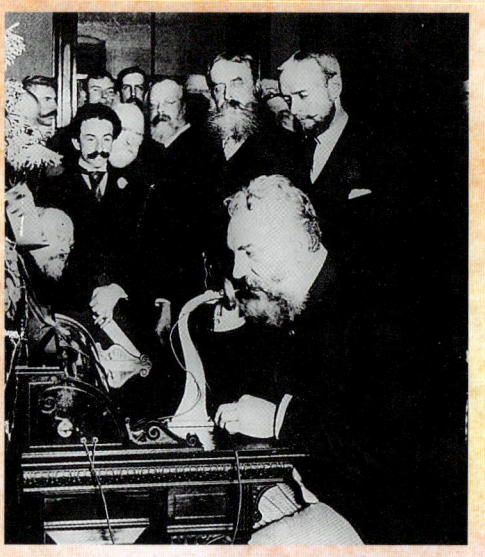

EARLY EXCHANGE

Early telephone exchanges were worked by people. To make a call, you pressed a button on your phone that connected you to the operator. The operator then connected you to the line you wanted. There were no individual telephone numbers. Female operators were preferred to males because they were more polite! The first telephone exchange was opened in the United States in 1878. It had just 21 lines.

An early telephone exchange

GET DIALING

The first phones with numbers and dials were introduced in the 1920s. These phones were linked to mechanical telephone exchanges. The exchange detected the number being dialed and made the connection automatically. Modern electronic exchanges are controlled by computer.

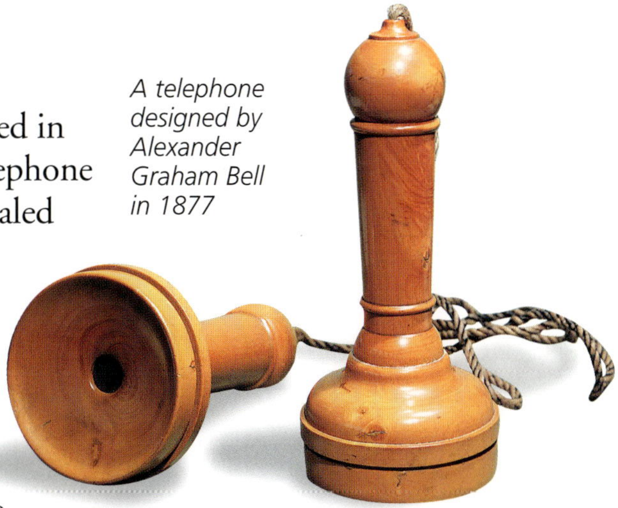

A telephone designed by Alexander Graham Bell in 1877

TRANSATLANTIC TELEPHONES

In 1956, a telephone line was laid across the Atlantic Ocean between Europe and North America. It could handle only 36 phone calls at a time. Today, more than a billion minutes of phone calls are made between Britain and the United States every year.

OPTICAL FIBERS

For many years, long-distance calls were sent through thick copper wires. In the 1960s a new type of "wire" was invented, called a fiber-optic cable. Each cable is made of very fine strands of glass. A caller's voice is turned into electrical signals, then into pulses of light that flash along the glass strands. Each strand is only the width of a human hair, yet it can carry thousands of phone calls at a time.

IN FACT...

The first automatic exchange was invented by an American undertaker in 1889. He was fed up with a rival undertaker who kept bribing the operators not to put through his calls!

The hair-thin strands of glass inside a fiber-optic cable

One of the first automatic dial telephones, dating from 1905. It was named after the American undertaker Almon B. Strowger.

On the Radio

The next great step forward in communications was to send messages without the use of wires. This was made possible with the invention of the radio, or wireless. A wireless set picked up signals that were sent through the air by invisible radio waves. This made it easier to communicate in places where it was difficult to lay cables – in mountainous areas, for example, or at sea.

Guglielmo Marconi (1874-1937)

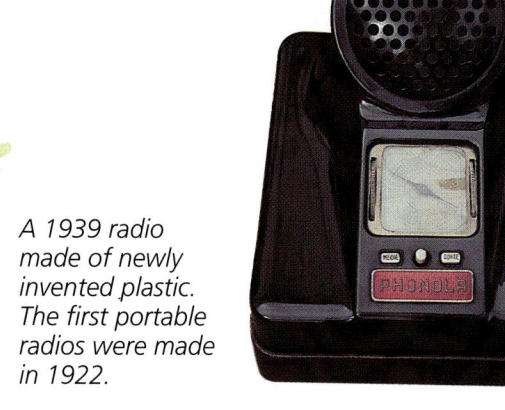

A 1939 radio made of newly invented plastic. The first portable radios were made in 1922.

RADIO PIONEERS

In 1888, a German scientist, Heinrich Hertz, proved that radio waves existed. But he could not find a practical use for them. In 1895, an Italian named Guglielmo Marconi began to experiment with using radio waves to send messages. He called his invention the wireless telegraph. It became better known as radio. Ships were quick to use the new radio. It meant, for the first time, that they could keep in touch with one another and with the shore even when they were out of sight. Before this, code flags had been their main means of communication (see page 8).

IN FACT...

In 1906 a Canadian physicist, Reginald A. Fessenden, attached a telephone mouthpiece to a wireless telegraph (radio) and began to transmit speech and other sounds for the first time. His first broadcast took place on December 24 and featured Christmas music and a reading from the Bible.

TELEVISION TAKES OVER

Television uses radio waves to send both sound and pictures. Although it has only been around for some 70 years, television has had a huge influence on our daily lives, bringing us news, sports, information, and entertainment from all parts of the globe. Today, more than 500 million homes around the world have television.

BREAKTHROUGH

In 1926, a Scottish engineer, John Logie Baird, gave the first demonstration of television in his London laboratory. The television showed the blurred picture of a boy's face. At first, Baird could not transmit sound and pictures at the same time. But by 1930, he was able to televise a 30-minute play from his studio.

Watching television in the 1940s. Early sets were large and bulky but had very small screens.

COLOR PICTURES

At first, television pictures were in black and white only. Color television began in the United States, when color pictures were transmitted in 1953. Color television started in Britain in the 1960s.

John Logie Baird at work on a color television receiver in his laboratory

BROADCAST RADIO

The radio you listen to is called broadcast radio. Instead of sending signals from one particular place to another, a radio station transmits signals, as sound and music, in all directions. These signals are picked up by your radio. The first radio stations started to broadcast news and entertainment in the early 1920s. By 1925, there were 600 stations worldwide. Today, the BBC World Service broadcasts from London in 41 languages to about 140 million listeners every year.

Transmitters at a radio station

TRANSISTORS

Early radios were quite large and bulky. But the invention, in 1948, of tiny electronic devices called transistors meant that much smaller and more compact radios could be made. By the 1960s, portable radios were all the rage.

Modern-day radios are often combined with audiotape cassette or CD players.

SIGNPOST

In the 1990s, a British inventor, Trevor Baylis, invented the clockwork radio. Instead of being powered by a battery, the radio works by winding a handle to generate electricity. It is ideal for poor or remote countries where batteries are costly and difficult to buy.

BROADCAST NEWS

The first television broadcasts were made in 1936 by the BBC (British Broadcasting Corporation). One of the very first programs was a demonstration of self-defense techniques. Broadcasts began in the United States in 1939. During World War II, there was no broadcasting. But by the 1950s, television stations had sprung up all over Europe and the United States. The first major television program to be broadcast internationally was the coronation of the British queen Elizabeth II, in 1953.

The coronation of Queen Elizabeth II was the first major event to be broadcast worldwide.

ON TAPE

Videotape recorders were developed in the 1950s to record pictures and sound on tape. At first, they were bulky and expensive, and they were used only by television stations. But in the 1970s smaller, cheaper videotape recorders were made for people to plug into their television sets at home. People could now record programs to watch whenever they wanted.

IN FACT...
The smallest television set was the TV-Wrist Watch, launched by the Japanese company Seiko in 1982. The tiny screen was just 1 inch (30 millimeters) square.

EARTH AND SPACE

Inside a modern TV studio

At a television station, pictures and sound are turned into electrical signals, then into radio waves that are transmitted to your home. Your television set picks up the radio waves, converts them into electrical signals, then changes the signals back into pictures and sound. This is called terrestrial (land) television. Another way of sending signals is by satellite (see page 24). Electrical signals can also be sent directly to your home along underground cables. This is called cable television.

23

MODERN COMMUNICATIONS

SATELLITES AND COMPUTERS

Using the latest satellite technology, people can now communicate to and from the remotest places on Earth. Computers have made modern communications faster than ever before. We may take fast, efficient communications for granted, yet many of these incredible advances have happened only in the last 50 years.

COMMUNICATIONS SATELLITES

Today, there are dozens of satellites in orbit around Earth, sending radio, telephone, and television signals across the globe. Signals are beamed up to the satellite from a transmitter on the ground. They are then beamed back down from the satellite to a receiver. The transmitter and receiver can be thousands of miles apart on Earth.

An astronaut guides a satellite into the space shuttle for repair.

BREAKTHROUGH

The first communications satellite was *Echo I* (below), launched in 1960. It looked like a giant metallic balloon. Until that time, there were no rockets powerful enough to launch satellites into orbit. Many modern satellites are now launched from the space shuttle. Astronauts can also recapture satellites in order to make repairs.

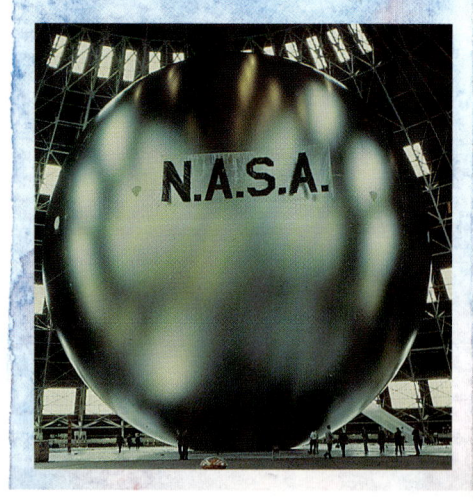

24

Using a mobile satellite to make a telephone call in a remote desert region. The white square is the antenna. The silver box contains the signal-processing equipment.

IN FACT...

When astronaut Neil Armstrong took his first steps on the moon in 1969, an estimated 600 million people were able to watch from their own homes. The pictures were sent back to the United States by cameras on board the lunar module. They were then beamed around the world by satellite.

LIVE TV

The *Telstar* satellite, launched in 1962, relayed the first live television pictures across the Atlantic Ocean. They were beamed from Maine to Cornwall, England, via *Telstar*. The broadcast lasted for just 20 minutes. *Telstar* could also carry up to 60 telephone calls. The latest satellites can receive and transmit more than 30,000 telephone calls and several television channels at the same time.

SURFING THE NET

In the last 30 years, computers have revolutionized the way we store and exchange information. A huge number of offices, homes, and schools now use computers. Sometimes a number of computers are linked together to form a computer network. The Internet (or Net) is the biggest computer network in the world. It connects thousands of smaller networks in universities and other organizations worldwide. The Internet began in the United States in 1984. You can use it to find and send information, play games, and communicate with people on the other side of the world by sending e-mail (electronic mail). Experts think that, in just 10 years' time, more than 500 million people will be linked up to the Net.

Anyone can go into a Cybercafé and log on to the Internet.

INTO THE FUTURE

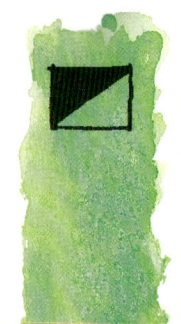

So, how will we communicate with one another in the future? The technology is constantly changing and improving. Will even more sophisticated machines take the place of telephones and televisions? They probably will. After all, until about 100 years ago, the very idea of telephones and television would have seemed much too far-fetched to be true.

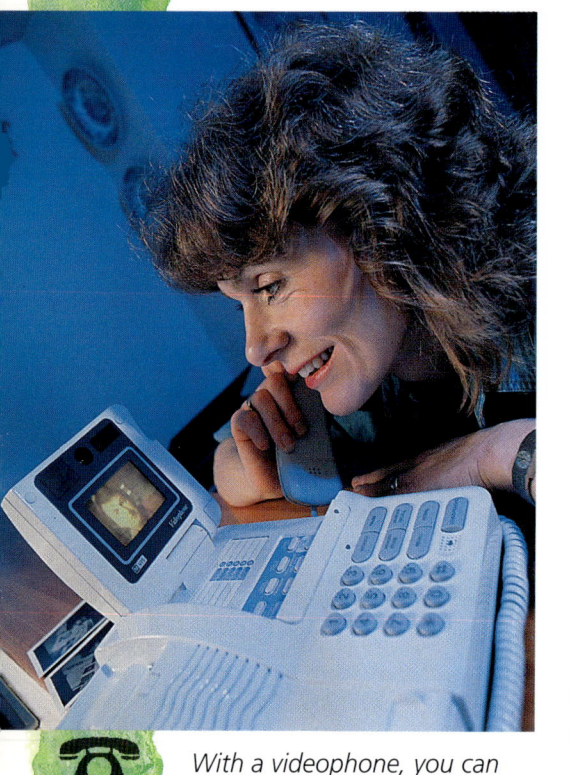

VIDEOPHONES

With a videophone, you can see the person to whom you are talking. A small camera videotapes you as you speak. The camera is attached to a computer that transmits speech, pictures, and text to the person you are calling. Videophones are already available to buy. But make sure the person you are calling has one, too!

INFORMATION SUPERHIGHWAY

Computers and communications networks have made it possible to send and receive huge amounts of information almost instantly, wherever you are in the world. In the future, more and more information will be sent through the Internet. This network for passing on information is known as the information superhighway.

With a videophone, you can see the person you are calling and he or she can see you. A small camera above the screen records your pictures and transmits them to the other user's screen.

You can use the Internet at home to access a huge range of information and to send messages around the world.

SIGNPOST

Would you like to watch television in 3-D (three dimensions)? You would be able to see all the way around people and objects, as if they were real. A hologram is a type of 3-D photograph. Holograms are made with very intense beams of light, called lasers. They are already used in medicine to produce 3-D images of the human body. One day, they may also be used to make 3-D films and television programs.

TELEPUTERS

A teleputer is a television and personal computer rolled into one. It can do everything a computer can do, such as processing information and accessing the Internet. It can also receive high-definition television pictures (HDTV). These are much clearer than ordinary pictures.

Teleconferencing is already used in many offices.

DISTANT CONFERENCING

Teleconferencing already provides a way for businesspeople to talk to each other without leaving their offices. In the future, they will be able to meet in a virtual world, created by a computer. To take part in a virtual conference, you have to wear a special headset. This makes everything in the conference room, including the other people, look three-dimensional. In the future, virtual reality will be used widely for many forms of communication. You will even be able to go virtual shopping!

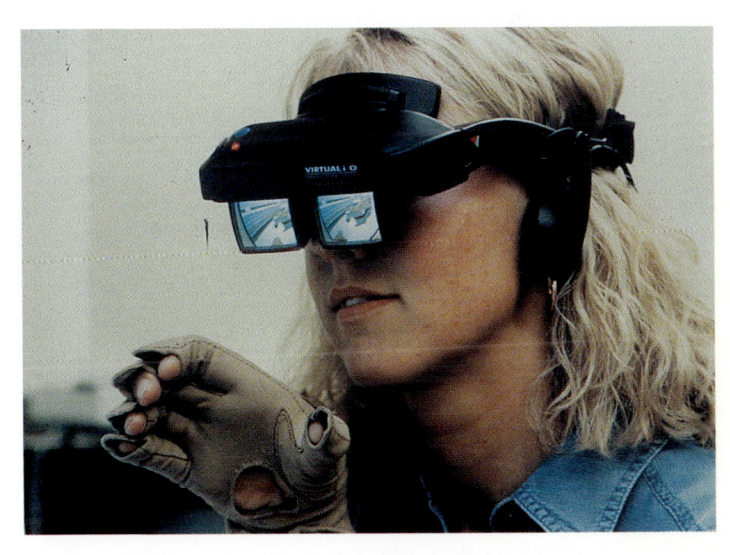

Instead of going to the supermarket, you can put on a virtual headset and go virtual shopping.

27

Timeline

B.C.
- *c.* **40,000** People start to use speech
- *c.* **3500** Writing begins in Sumeria
- **1st century** Roman postal system established

A.D.
- **1040** The Chinese invent movable type
- **1438** Printing press invented in Europe
- **1627** First public post offices open in France
- **1790s** Mechanical telegraph invented
- **1830s** Photography becomes more practical
- **1840** First stick-on postage stamps issued
- **1843** World's first public telegraph service installed in England
- **1844** Morse code invented
- **1860** Pony Express begins in the United States
- **1876** First telephone call made by Alexander Graham Bell
- **1878** First telephone exchange opens in the United States
- **1887** Esperanto (a universal language) is invented
- **1896** Guglielmo Marconi invents radio
- **1906** First radio broadcast
- **1919** First regular airmail service begins
- **1926** First demonstration of television by John Logie Baird
- **1936** First television broadcasts in Britain
- **1939** First television broadcasts in the United States
- **1948** Invention of transistors
- **1953** Color television begins in the United States
- **1960** First communications satellite launched
- **1960s** Fiber-optic cables invented
- **1965** The *Earlybird* satellite carries phone calls across the Atlantic
- **1970s** Home videotape recorders available
- **1980s** Fax machines become popular
- **1980s** Mobile phones become available
- **1984** The Internet begins in the United States
- **1990s** Invention of the clockwork radio

GLOSSARY

Airmail Mail that is carried by aircraft, to even the remotest parts of the world.

Cable television Television in which the sound and picture signals reach your home through a cable under the ground.

Code A way of sending messages, often secret messages, using signs or symbols to stand for words and letters.

E-mail Short for "electronic mail". E-mail is a way of sending messages from one computer to another via a computer network.

Esperanto A universal language, invented in 1887. It is based on a mixture of Latin, Greek, German, and Italian.

Fiber-optic cable A cable made up of hair-thin fibers that carry telephone or television signals as flashes of light.

High-definition television (HDTV) A new form of television that gives a better picture. A television picture is made up of hundreds of horizontal lines. An HDTV picture is clearer because it is made up of more lines than usual.

Hologram A three-dimensional photograph created using lasers (strong beams of light).

Information superhighway The network through which electronic data is transmitted around the world.

Internet The Internet, or Net, is the largest computer network in the world, made up of thousands of smaller networks and with some 100 million users worldwide.

Modem Stands for "modulator/demodulator." A device that allows computer data to be sent across a telephone line.

Morse code A code of dots and dashes devised by Samuel Morse in 1844. Different combinations of dots and dashes stand for different letters and numbers.

Pony Express A postal service set up in the United States in the mid-19th century. Letters were carried by teams of riders on horseback.

Radio A way of sending messages without the use of wires. Instead, signals are sent through the air by invisible radio waves.

Satellite A manufactured object that orbits Earth. A communications satellite transmits telephone and television signals around the world.

Satellite television Television in which the sound and picture signals reach your home via a satellite in space.

Telecommunications Ways of sending messages using electricity. They include the telegraph, the telephone, radio, and television.

Telegram A message sent by telegraph.

Telegraph A machine that sends letters and words along a wire or wires in the form of an electrical code.

Telephone exchange Where your call is connected to the number you are dialing. Modern exchanges are operated automatically, by computer.

Transistor An electronic device that turns an electric current on and off, or strengthens an electric current.

Virtual reality A world created by computer that gives the impression of being real.

Wireless Another name for a radio.

Index

ancient China 12
ancient Egyptians 12
ancient Greeks 8, 12
animal communications 9
Armstrong, Neil 25
Assyrians 12
Augustus, Emperor 12

Battle of Trafalgar 8
Bayliss, Trevor 21
BBC World Service 21
Bell, Alexander Graham 18, 19

cameras 6
cave painting 7
Chappe, Claude 16
codes 9
 Morse code 6
computers 7, 24, 25, 26
 e-mail 25
 information superhighway 26
 Internet 25, 26, 27

de l'Epée, Charles 9
dictionaries 11

electricity, discovery of 6
Esperanto 11

Fessenden, Reginald A. 20
flags 8
 code flags 8, 20
 Olympic flag 8
flight, invention of, 15

Hertz, Heinrich 20
holograms 27

Incas 13

Johnson, Samuel 11

languages 10, 11
 body language 9
 first speakers 10
 most spoken 10
 sign language 9
 silbo (whistle language) 11

Marconi, Guglielmo 20
Morse, Samuel 16

Nelson, Lord 8
newspapers 6

optical fibers 16, 19

photography 6
pigeon mail 12
Pony Express 14
postage stamps 15
 Penny Black 15
postal services 12, 13
 animal services 15
 cursus publicus (Roman) 12
 first public 14
 biggest 14
printing 6
 invention of 13

radio 16, 20, 21
 clockwork 21
 first broadcast 20
 first portable 20, 21
 first radio stations 21
Romans 8, 12

satellites 7, 24, 25
 Echo I 24
 Telstar 25
signals 8, 9
 with mirrors 8
steam transportation 14
symbols 8, 9

technological breakthroughs 6
telecommunications 7, 16, 17
teleconferencing 27
telegrams 17
telegraph 16, 17
 electric telegraph 16
 first public telegraph 17
 invention of 16
 mechanical telegraph 16
telephone 16, 18, 19
 automatic exchanges 19
 electronic exchanges 19
 first exchanges 18, 19
 first phone call 18
 mobile phones 7
 video phones 26
teleputers 27
television 16, 22, 23
 cable television 23
 color television 22
 first broadcasts 23
 first pictures 22
 HDTV (high-definition TV) 27
 satellite television 7, 23
 smallest sets 23
 terrestrial television 23
torch messages 8
Tower of Babel 10
transistors 21

video recording 23
virtual reality 27
 virtual conferencing 27

writing 6, 10

Zamenhof, Ludwig 11